A Sadler's Wells, Theat
& Kneehigh

TANIKA GUPTA

WAH! WAH! GIRLS THE MUSICAL
BRITAIN MEETS BOLLYWOOD

In association with Hall for Cornwall

Part of World Stages London
Funded by Arts Council England & British Council
Research supported by Jerwood Studio at Sadler's Wells

OBERON BOOKS
LONDON

WWW.OBERONBOOKS.COM

First published in 2012 by Oberon Books Ltd
521 Caledonian Road, London N7 9RH
Tel: +44 (0) 20 7607 3637 / Fax: +44 (0) 20 7607 3629
e-mail: info@oberonbooks.com
www.oberonbooks.com

A catalogue record for this book is available from the British Library.

PB ISBN: 978-1-84943-187-3
Digital ISBN: 978-1-84943-631-1

Cover:
Image of solo dancer Payal Patel
by Hugo Glendinning
Design by snowcreative.co.uk

Printed, bound and converted
by CPI Group (UK) Ltd, Croydon, CR0 4YY.

Visit www.oberonbooks.com to read more about all our books
and to buy them. You will also find features, author interviews and
news of any author events, and you can sign up for e-newsletters
so that you're always first to hear about our new releases.

This play is dedicated to my Wah! Wah! Girls
Nandini, Niku and Malini

Characters

(In order of appearance)

BINDI
TV/couch potato – Indian woman

SORAYA
Asian woman in her late forties.

KABIR
Asian man in his early twenties.
Soraya's son.

ANITA
Young Mujra girl

SHANTI
Young Mujra girl

FAUZIA
Young Mujra girl

MANSOOR
Elderly Asian shopkeeper

PAVEL
A Polish builder

CAL
Afro-Caribbean man in his late forties.
Soraya's next-door neighbour.

SITA
17-year-old Asian woman from Leeds

ANISH / TARIQ
30-year-old Asian men

SAMEENA BIBI
Madame of Indian Mujra

OMAR
Dancer in Mujra. Early 20s

DEVI
A winged magical goddess. Indian singer.

Ensemble parts
Dancers

Wah! Wah! Girls premiered on 24 May 2012 at the Peacock Theatre, London, before touring to Theatre Royal Stratford East and Hall for Cornwall with the following cast:

BINDI / SAMEENA BIBI	Rina Fatania
SORAYA	Sophiya Haque
KABIR	Tariq Jordan
ANITA	Davina Perera
SHANTI / YOUNG SORAYA	Sheena Patel
FAUZIA	Shelley Williams
MANSOOR	Tony Jayawardena
PAVEL	Philip Brodie
CAL	Delroy Atkinson
SITA	Rebecca Grant
	Natasha Jayetileke
ANISH / TARIQ	Gurpreet Singh
OMAR	Keeza Farhan
DEVI	Japjit Kaur

Creative Team

Book and Lyrics Tanika Gupta

Music Niraj Chag

Director Emma Rice

Associate Director Pravesh Kumar

Bollywood Choreographer Javed Sanadi

Kathak Choreographer Gauri Sharma Tripathi

Set & Costume Design Keith Khan

Lighting Design Malcolm Rippeth

Sound Design Simon Baker

Musical Director Mark Collins

Associate Musical Director Tom Brady

Musical Consultant Nigel Lilley

Dramaturgy Paul Sirett

SCENE 1

An Asian pensioner, BINDI enters carrying a large bowl of crisps. She flops down in a tatty old armchair and aims her remote control at TV screen. As she flicks through the channels, nothing catches her eye.

(NB. BINDI represents our TV viewer. She appears in every scene, sometimes sitting in the corner in her tatty armchair, other times joining in. In a sense, she is our point of view.)

We hear/see the assortment of programmes: a football match, an OTT Australian soap, a gyrating pop video, a period drama, gunshots of a cops and robbers and car chase, a wildlife programme etc. BINDI looks bored.

Suddenly SORAYA's face comes on screen. BINDI's finger hovers over the remote button. She is transfixed. As the camera shot is close-up on SORAYA, we only see her face, but we and BINDI can see SORAYA as she speaks gently and beguilingly into the camera.

SORAYA: Good evening Bindi Shah.

> *BINDI looks startled.*

Yes, I'm talking to you. Please put down your Bombay mix.

> *BINDI quickly does as she is told.*

Thank you so much for coming along today. It is delightful to see all of you. Some old faces and some new ones. Welcome to you all. Accept my *salaams*, my *namastes* and of course my 'how do you dos'.

SORAYA steps through the screen and emerges, standing in BINDI's space. She looks bemused but gazes up at her adoringly.

SORAYA is dressed exquisitely in silk brocade but is not too flashy. She smiles and addresses the audience. She is well-spoken charming and accomplished.

The audience cheers, BINDI looks around her, startled as she notices a few people have entered her lounge and are settling down on cushions, lounging around her on the floor.

BINDI happily settles back in her chair and puts down the remote.

She calls out.

BINDI: Wah! Wah!

Three beautiful young women, suitably bedecked as Indian dancing girls in bright silks and jewellery, with bells on the ankles burst through the screen.

WAH! WAH! GIRLS SONG IN HINDI
Aaj ki shaam, has bus tumhare naam
Is haseen mehfil ka tumko salaam
Husn Aur adaa ka aisa hai ye jahaan
Aaye jo bhi yahaan ho jaaye fida

Vah vah kahe ye saara jahaan
Jab bhi ye ghungaroo baje yahaan
Inki adaao mein hai aisa nasha
Ke vah vah Kare ye saara jahaan

Translation –
Tonight is in your name
Accept the welcome/hello of this beautiful gathering
This is the world of intoxicating Beauty
Whoever comes here falls in love with it (head over heels)

Vah vah says the whole world
Whenever you hear the sound of ghungaroos here
Such is the charm of these anklet bells
That vah vah says the whole world

BINDI jumps up and addresses the dancers.

BINDI: Life has been terrifically hard for us. Bills, cars, kids, job losses, everything's so expensive and now these bloody Olympics taking over the city. It's a tough time for everyone and all of us are struggling to keep our heads above water.

Bring us one love! True love! Big love!

Wah! Wah!

It is something to rouse the rabble, show off the dancers' different dancing skills and to set the audience on fire. The dance is more traditional classical-style dance, not Bollywood but more based on kathak and thumris. But it is highly entertaining and visual. This opening dance should be full of joy and fun.

The audience on the stage are not passive but appreciative, both verbally and physically. In the traditional way of a Mujra audience, they call out –

AUDIENCE: *Wah-Wah!*

They salaam the dancers, cheer at a particularly skilful moment in the dance and sometimes even get up to shout their appreciation. BINDI happily joins in, delighted with the TV show and hands her bowl of crisps around.

At the end of the dance, everyone disappears back through the screen leaving BINDI on her own. She puts on her coat and heads out to the shops.

SCENE 2

Music as the scene opens in the East End of London.

We recreate the hustle and bustle of an East End main street first thing in the morning as BINDI walks through.

We see: White youths, women in hijabs carrying their briefcases, pushing their babies, power dressed, low life, down and outs, flash Harries, high-heeled beauties, and ordinary folk go about their daily lives.

We see two halal butchers with their prayer caps on unloading a large carcass and carrying it through to their shop.

We see a couple of Polish builders hanging about in their work clothes. This scene should be full of the vibrancy and colour of the city.

BINDI exits her house and bumps into PAVEL.

PAVEL: Morning Bindi.

BINDI: Ah. Pavel. Looking very handsome today.

PAVEL: Thank you! And you are wearing a very fetching cardigan today.

BINDI: Ohh – this old thing…

PAVEL: You know how I keep looking so good? I have a secret for youth.

BINDI: Really? Tell me!

PAVEL: Cheap and simple.

BINDI: Tell me!

PAVEL: I wear it every day on my face.

BINDI: What?

PAVEL: A big, broad smile.

BINDI: Ahhh – very good. Very good.

PAVEL: It keeps me young. Although a good moisturiser helps too…

Everything good with you?

BINDI: My television is on the blink.

PAVEL: On the blink?

BINDI: Not working very well. Changing channels and…old man is away…usually fixing things is his department.

PAVEL: I can fix it for you.

BINDI: Erm…

PAVEL: You should give your husband some rest and let me help you. I can fix your taps, your gutters, I do carpentry, kitchen fitting, plastering, rubbish clearance, painting, decorating…any place, any time, anywhere, twenty-four hours a day, Pavel is at your service.

BINDI: It's okay. I have a lot of work to do – shouldn't be wasting my time goggle eyes in front of the box.

PAVEL: I think it's your satellite dish. I noticed earlier there are pigeons up there.

BINDI: Those horrid birds are everywhere!

PAVEL: Millions in London. You know, they can live up to thirty-five years?

BINDI: Hai! Hai! They are planning pigeon world domination! In our Hindu religion, they are the messengers for Yama – the God of Death. They give me the heebie jeebies.

PAVEL: Heebie jeebies?

BINDI: You know, colly wobbles.

PAVEL: Colly…?

BINDI: Spine tingling… Shivers…

PAVEL: Ah! You mean when the hairs on your back stand up and your heart is pounding in your mouth?

BINDI: Exactly. Pigeons of death.

BINDI looks up at the sky with fear.

PAVEL: Maybe, there is a nest. I tell you what, I bring ladder, I go up there. Pigeons don't scare me. Never fear, Pavel is here.

BINDI: It's fine. I'll ask Cal. He will do it for me.

PAVEL looks upset.

PAVEL: Cal, Cal, always Cal.

BINDI: Don't be angry Pavel. But Cal is old friend. I can't be unfaithful to him.

PAVEL: You know, there is a saying in Poland: Lover's have a right to betray you – but friends don't.

PAVEL exits. BINDI looks guilty.

Situated in the middle of this is the shop front of a small dry cleaners: 'DELUXE-DHOBI-WALLAH' (Washerman). MANSOOR – an older man is sweeping up the broken glass. A postman hands him some mail, he opens the letters and groans (Bills).

MANSOOR'S SONG – 'Yah Allah!'

1.
I used to dream of golden pavements
But instead I found enslavement
Jobs below me – neighbours all so rude –
Worked all hours just for rent and food.

2.
I hate this town – this sprawl
Stinking rotten from decline and fall
Chancers, drifters, hustlers, gangsters,
Whores and tarts and thugs and thieves.

CHORUS

Yah Allah!

Thirty years of blood and sweat
Yah Allah!
Fingers worn away and endless debt
Yah Allah!
There is no hope, this world is hell.
This is my f-a-t-e.

Yah Allah!
Thirty years of sweat and tears
Yah Allah!
My laundry shop fed us down the years
My sons have grown and all gone now
Left me to my f-a-t-e.

PAVEL *(the Polish builder) enters – stops and surveys the damage.*

PAVEL: *(Polish Accent.)* Mansoor! Another break-in?

MANSOOR: Fourth one this year.

PAVEL: They take anything?

MANSOOR: No, Allah is merciful. The alarm went off and the cowards scarpered. Fourth time this year though.

PAVEL: You want I fix it for you? Very reasonable rates.

MANSOOR: It's okay, thanks. Cal's doing it for me.

PAVEL: Always Cal. You should try me out for a change.

PAVEL waves and goes on his way.

MANSOOR: *(Mutters.)* Bloody Poles, taking all our jobs. Go back to your own country!

SONG:

MANSOOR:

3.
What thanks or joy for me?
No respect from my community?
Pay my taxes, say my prayers
No one left to share my cares.

(CHORUS RPT.)

CAL, a middle-aged Afro-Caribbean man dressed in his work clothes approaches the shop.

CAL: Good morning Mansoor.

MANSOOR: Good? What's good about it Cal?

CAL: Aww…c'mon – it's just a broken shop front. Hazards of the job – and you're insured.

MANSOOR: With my premiums going through the roof! This area is going down the drain…to the dogs! Look at this mess.

CAL: I've already ordered the glass. It'll be here this afternoon fixed for you in no time. You called the Police?

MANSOOR: I called and called and called again. They don't care. They say they will try and drop by…'later'.

CAL: Cheer up old man.

MANSOOR: Look up there.

CAL looks up and smiles.

MANSOOR: What do you see?

CAL: The big, wide open sky and an airplane flying to…
Barbados? St Lucia?
What do you see?

MANSOOR: Grey skies, impenetrable thick smog,
hanging over us like a blanket of cement.

CAL laughs and shakes his head.

ANITA, SHANTI and FAUZIA all walk past. They eye the broken glass and look at MANSOOR. MANSOOR scowls at them all. SHANTI scurries on, FAUZIA stops right in front of MANSOOR.

FAUZIA: Oh girls, wait. Whoops, I've just dropped my oyster card.

She bends over provocatively right under MANSOOR's nose.

Found it!

ANITA and SHANTI cat call.

ANITA: Kiss my Chuddies

SHANTI: Bottoms up!

ANITA: Yo Girl! Your arse is mint!

As the girls exit.

MANSOOR continues his song:

'Yah Allah'

4.
Dancing girls I see them lure
Weak willed men into their evil lair
Fallen women, wasted lives
A world of lust and lies

(CHORUS RPT.)

CAL: Oh stop your whingeing.

MANSOOR: Those women bring the area down.

CAL: You're taking out your frustrations on innocent women. They're just trying to earn a living.

MANSOOR: It's a brothel!

CAL: It's a dancing club!

MANSOOR: Home wreckers! They should be shut down and kicked out.

CAL: Live and let live Mansoor.

MANSOOR: Cal, you're a good man. A good neighbour and a loyal friend. But don't you see, these women are evil?

CAL: You're just in a bad mood because your windows were smashed. Now lighten up Manny, before the poison in your head spills out and seeps into your heart.

CAL throws up his hands in frustration and exits.

As CAL exits, SITA arrives on the bus. BINDI watches her with interest as SITA jumps off and looks around her with a mixture of delight and amazement. MANSOOR is still sweeping up the glass in front of his shop. SITA approaches him.

SITA: Good morning Uncle!

She sees BINDI.

Auntie.

MANSOOR stops sweeping and scowls at SITA. He pushes BINDI away.

MANSOOR: What's good about it?

SITA: It's a lovely day isn't it? By the way – name's Sita.

SITA grins and sticks out her hand to shake hands with MANSOOR. He looks at her hand suspiciously. Instead he salaams her. SITA smartly salaams him back.

MANSOOR: Not from around here are you?

SITA: No…I'm visiting friends…in fact I was wondering if you could help me Uncle. I'm looking for an address.

SITA pulls out a scrap of paper from her bag.

MANSOOR: Do I look like an A to Z to you?

SITA is amazed by MANSOOR's rudeness

SITA: Alright Uncle. Who rattled your cage?

MANSOOR: I am not your uncle and as you can see, I am busy, sweeping up because my shop has been vandalised.

SITA: I'm sorry for your troubles. But please – just help me out will you? I know it's around here some place. It's a dancing club called 'Wah! Wah! Girls.'

MANSOOR: I don't frequent places like that and I suggest you don't either. Very disreputable and not a place for young girls. Take my advice Sita, go home and leave me in peace.

SITA turns away angrily and exits.

SITA: Suit yourself. Sorry to have bothered you, 'uncle'.

BINDI looks at MANSOOR and shakes her head.

BINDI: Grumpy old git.

BINDI beckons SITA to her and gives her directions.

BINDI: Turn left, then right, then walk straight, then look left and right and then right again before crossing the road carefully. Don't go into the chicken shop – very bad people there – Turn around and it's straight ahead of you.

SITA looks confused.

SITA: Auntie? Do you mean it's just across the road?

BINDI nods.

SCENE 3

BINDI settles down in her armchair and watches the scene unfold. She is still clutching her remote control.

The scene opens in SORAYA's home. SORAYA sits bored at a table, sorting through bills, peering through her reading specs and clicking away on her laptop. KABIR, her son, paces up and down in front of her.

SORAYA: Bollywood lap-dancing? Bollywood wedding-planning? Bollywood makeover sessions? Dance classes? Asian stag nights?

KABIR: Yes! We have to diversify.

SORAYA: Why?

KABIR: Because the act is too…old-fashioned.

SORAYA: So what? People still come to watch my 'old-fashioned' girls.

KABIR: But not as many come.

SORAYA: That's because of the recession.

KABIR: You can see for yourself, we can't pay the bills.

SORAYA: Yes, we're definitely short this month.

KABIR: And last month, and the month before…

SORAYA: We have a big household. Too many mouths to feed. Maybe we should get rid of one of them.

KABIR: I didn't say we should get rid of anyone.
But if we ran this properly – in a more business-like way, then we'd be able to make a profit.

SORAYA: Why are you getting so hysterical *beta*?
We've managed before.

KABIR: This feels more serious. Like…

SORAYA: Please stop worrying. In fact, for a young man, you worry far too much. You should be going out, changing girlfriends like socks. When was the last time you even had a girlfriend?

KABIR: Mum!

SORAYA: Nineteen years old and already the weight of the world is on your shoulders.

KABIR: I'm 21!

SORAYA: Shhh… You stay young, I stay young…

KABIR: You've managed to change the subject again!

We see a young woman (SITA) breaking in to a room upstairs.

KABIR: Mum, we've got to do something, otherwise we're going to go under.

SORAYA: I'm not holding you captive here. I want you to go out there and find a life, a love, have children! Why are you still hanging around your mother? That is a little 'old-fashioned' isn't it?

KABIR: You want me to go?

SORAYA: No. But I don't think you should interfere with the running of my business. If you want to do all this Bollywood Bullshit – then by all means – go and do it. I'm not stopping you.

KABIR: Maybe I will go then.

SORAYA: Maybe you should.

SHANTI, FAUZIA and ANITA enter with shopping bags.

ALL: We're back Soraya Bibi

SHANTI and FAUZIA exit.

ANITA: Soraya Bibi –
Looks like Mansoor had his shop
window kicked in again.

SORAYA: Serves him right.

ANITA: I feel sorry for Mansoor. He virtually lives in that shop.

SORAYA: Don't feel sorry for him. He's a bad tempered old goat. His wife left him after their three sons left home. He drove them all away. Let him fester in that stinking hole he calls a shop.

KABIR looks at his mother, amused.

SORAYA: What's that look for?

KABIR: Nothing.

SORAYA: Don't you dare compare me to Mansoor.

KABIR: I didn't say anything!

There is a commotion in the back/g. We hear the excited clamour of women.

SITA: *(Off stage.)* Let me go…stop pushing me!

FAUZIA: *(Off stage.)* Soraya Bibi! Soraya Bibi!

SHANTI: *(Off stage.)* Look!

Enter OMAR, FAUZIA and SHANTI. They look excited as they drag a frightened young woman (in her late teens) into the room, SITA.

SORAYA: What's going on?

FAUZIA: We've had an intruder Soraya Bibi!

SHANTI: She broke in!

OMAR: Anita, you left your window open – again.

ANITA: Oops.

SORAYA stands and looks, worried.

SITA: Get your dirty hands off me. Let go. I can explain…!

FAUZIA: Soraya Bibi? Shall we call the Police?

SITA: I…I…I…

SORAYA: How dare you break in to my home.

Who are you?

SITA: My name's Sita. I'm running away from home and I want to work here.

SORAYA: Running away? Omar, call her parents.

OMAR *pulls out his phone.*

SITA: No! Please!

SORAYA: How old are you?

SITA: Seventeen.

SORAYA: For God's sake. We'll have her whole extended family down here banging on the doors. Get rid of her Kabir.

KABIR: Hold on… *(KABIR is more gentle.)*
Sita, How come you're running away? Won't your parents be worried?

SITA: It's not safe for me at home.

SORAYA: The more you tell me the more I don't want to know. Now get out and don't come back or I *will* call the Police.

KABIR: Mum, hear her out.

SITA: My brother – he won't let me do anything I want. Taken me out of college, won't let me finish my education.

KABIR: That's awful.

SITA: I've got nowhere else to go. They're trying to hunt me down. I've got to hide…

SORAYA: I'm sorry, but I fail to understand what that's got to do with me. Why come here? This is a dance club not a women's refuge.

KABIR: Mum! For God's sake!

SITA: I want to learn to dance from you. I can sing too.

SORAYA: I feel sorry for you, I really do. But I can't help you.

FAUZIA: How did you know about this place?

SITA: My cousin Sheena, told my mate Rina whose aunty Davina used to dance here. Everyone talks about this club. I've always wanted to dance.

SORAYA: And my son here wanted to be a rocket scientist, but that didn't mean he turned up at NASA.

SHANTI: Soraya Bibi…

OMAR: We need an extra dancer.

KABIR: Yeah mum, at least try her out.

SORAYA: *(Relents reluctantly.)* Go on then. Let's hear you.

SITA: Now?

SORAYA: Here and now. Or else, I'll show you the door. One thing I have learnt through the years is that sentimentality gets you nowhere.

SITA looks very self-conscious and shuffles from one foot to the other.

SORAYA: Is that it?

SITA: No. Wait. Please.

SITA grabs a CD from her bag. BINDI puts the CD on for her.

SITA starts to sing. As she does, we see CAL peeking in through a window.

Her voice is shaky to begin with, but as she warms up, her voice is clear and passionate. Soon, her singing and dancing takes over. It is a raunchy number which captivates everyone who is watching her. KABIR is particularly smitten.

SONG 'CHOLI KE PECCHE KYA-HAI'
FROM THE FILM: KHALNAYAK (1993)

What is under your blouse?
What is under your shawl?
My heart is in my blouse
My heart is under my shawl
This heart I will give to my friend
To my beloved
Save me, my dear, save me
The crazed lovers are after me
Someone is pulling me
What should I do? What should I do?

At the end of the song, all eyes turn to SORAYA who tries to hide the fact that she is impressed.

SORAYA: You can dance, but the style is a little…for my tastes…too suggestive.

SITA looks disappointed.

SORAYA: Fauzia, show Sita to the back bedroom. Anita, give her something to eat and Shanti, will you get some fresh linen from the cupboards. And Omar, you can't borrow her dress and you wouldn't fit into her blouse.

SITA: Thank you Soraya Bibi.

SORAYA looks away and sees CAL at the window.

The young women all leave the room, very excited.

KABIR: She was magic.

SORAYA: Like a 'Bollywood lap dancer' eh Kabir? Right up your street.
That girl has the scent of trouble hanging about her. What are you grinning about Cal?

CAL: You.

He mimics SORAYA.

CAL: 'One thing I have learnt through the years is that sentimentality gets you nowhere'.

Both CAL and KABIR laugh.

BINDI laughs out loud as well.

SCENE 4

SITA is shown into her small room with a bed. The other girls (ANITA, SHANTI and FAUZIA) crowd around her. SITA looks around the room, shy and tentative.

ANITA: Where are you from?

SITA: Leeds.

SHANTI: You dance beautifully.

SITA: Thank you.

SHANTI: Just like Madhuri.

FAUZIA: Give me a break. Madhuri Dixit?

ANITA: Fauzia!

FAUZIA: She can dance yes – but comparing her to Madhuri is going too far.

SHANTI: Did you see the way Kabir was looking at her?

ANITA and SHANTI laugh.

ANITA: He was struck dumb.

SHANTI: Like the whole world stopped for a moment.
Love at first sight.

SITA: *(Smiles.)* He was kinda cute.

The girls all exclaim.

FAUZIA: Better watch out though, he is the apple of Soraya Bibi's eye. I wouldn't want her as my mother-in-law.

SITA: I didn't say I wanted to marry him.

SHANTI: But you like him.

SITA: He seems cool.

FAUZIA: Kabir ain't cool.

ANITA: Ohhh… He is sweet though.

SITA: Yeah, he was sweet to me.

FAUZIA: What's she like? She's here for two minutes and she's lusting after the landlady's son.

SITA: I'm not interested in any of that. I just want to keep my head down and work hard.

FAUZIA: Ahhh… Your boyfriend ditched you?

SITA: I don't have a boyfriend.

ANITA: Take no notice of Fauzia. She can be a bitch sometimes.

SHANTI: You mean most of the time.

FAUZIA: I'm a realist.

SHANTI: But Kabir is a lovely boy.

SITA: If you like him so much, why don't you go for him?

SHANTI: Kabir?! He's more like a brother to us!

SITA: Then, he can be my brother too.

FAUZIA: I don't think he wants to be your brother…if you get what I mean.

SITA: What's *she* like?

FAUZIA: Soraya Bibi?

SITA: I thought she were a bit scary.

SHANTI: She's very strict.

SITA: What's it like living here?

ANITA: We have to dance day and night.

SHANTI: When we're not dancing, we're rehearsing.

FAUZIA: When we're not rehearsing, we're cleaning.

ANITA: When we're not cleaning, we're making our dance costumes.

FAUZIA: Or running errands for Soraya Bibi.

ANITA: She has a terrible temper.

SHANTI: Sometimes she hits us with a stick.

FAUZIA: And sometimes she forces us to 'entertain' the clients for money.

SITA looks horrified.

SITA: I – I thought it was just a place you could learn to dance.

The three girls all laugh at SITA. SITA picks up her bag and turns to leave.

ANITA: You muppet!

FAUZIA: That was too easy.

SHANTI: Come back!

ANITA: We're sorry.

FAUZIA: You're staying with us.

ANITA, SHANTI and FAUZIA sing and dance the 'Wah! Wah! Girls' song. This is a song and dance moment, with ANITA, SHANTI and FAUZIA leaping on the bed and bouncing around SITA. SITA watches and then joins in at the end.

WAH! WAH! GIRLS

1.
Look at you, your face full of fear
London town can be tough
the crowds rush on by
No time for words,
Your swollen eyes veiled with tears
This city weighing you down
with shrouds of grey sky

CHORUS

Wah! Wah! They call as we dance and we sing
Ghungrus ringing, bodies swaying
hands show love's glory, eyes burn our yearning
Dazzling, twirling, love-defining.

Wah! Wah! They call as we dance and we sing
Ghungrus ringing, bodies swaying
eyes set hearts racing, smiles bring men gasping
Whirling freely, life-affirming.

2.
You fled from the lies now your destiny's cast
You've broken all of your ties, free now at last,
Lost some you loved, your heart full of cries
Safe now at least but the world seems so vast.

REPEAT CHORUS

SCENE 5

BINDI enters a busy coffee shop, buys a coffee and sits and sips it.

CAL and SORAYA are sat close by. General hubbub around them.

SORAYA: Why are you fixing his shop front?

CAL: Because he asked me to.

SORAYA: I hope he's paying you.

CAL: That's my business.

SORAYA: I don't know what you see in that horrible man.

CAL: He's a good friend.

SORAYA: I'm a good friend.

CAL: Then you should know not to interfere in my other friendships.

SORAYA: He's a hateful, evil old man. He's been campaigning to close me down for years!

CAL: I know.

SORAYA: And you agree with him?

CAL: Each to their own Soraya.

SORAYA: What's that meant to mean?

CAL: Let's just drink our coffee and chill for a bit.

SORAYA: You are so laid back, you're almost horizontal.

CAL: Someone's got to keep the peace.
    Cal, can I ask you something? You never come to the club.

CAL: Not my kind of thing – dancing girls.

SORAYA: It's not Spearmint Rhinos. Do you think that somehow you're being unfaithful to your late wife – Venetia?

CAL: No. It's not that…she's been gone seven years now.

SORAYA: You still think about her?

CAL: All the time.

SORAYA: And you never met another woman since she died?

CAL: I met plenty of women.

SORAYA: But no one that compares?

CAL: I wouldn't say that.

SORAYA: Cal! It's like trying to get blood out of a stone!

CAL: What about you Soraya? What happened to Kabir's father? Where's he?

SORAYA: Long gone. Died when Kabir was a baby.

CAL: And you never met another man since he died?

SORAYA: I met plenty of men.

CAL and SORAYA grin at each other.

CAL: Touché.

SORAYA: As our local handyman – you know everyone's secrets around here don't you?

CAL: Yep, I get to see the whole spectrum of life.

SORAYA: Spill the beans.

CAL: I'm no gossip.

SORAYA: Come on.

CAL beckons SORAYA mischievously closer.

CAL: Look over there – Big Mr Singh
Best beware, the baron of bling

SORAYA: He gives us Asians a bad name.

CAL: He has the merc, fat diamond rings
They say 'round here his money sings
Landlord and loan shark, dealer in drugs
Sad feeble man – depends on thugs.

SORAYA: Drugs, really? Hypocrite. He's always bad-mouthing my club!

CAL points to another young man.

31

CAL: Young banker Joe – he had no shame
　　Five birds at once – or so he claimed
　　He said that love was just a game
　　They played along – tied him in chains.

SORAYA: Serves the bugger right!

CAL: Three days he was bound and gagged
　　Since then his libido's sagged.

SORAYA laughs delighted. CAL points to another man.

　　And over there, old bigot Stan.

SORAYA: Nasty piece of work.

CAL: Denies he has a Jewish gran
　　Hates poles, hates blacks, hates any tan
　　Whites rule he says, he's English man
　　But all his sons have chosen mates
　　That will dilute his precious race.

SORAYA: Excellent.
　　Now, how about you?

CAL: Me?

SORAYA: What's your story Cal?

CAL: I'm nobody special

SORAYA: Everyone's special.

CAL'S SONG 'I Love This Town'

1.

A crumbling mother England
Called my people to her land
They blew in with the Windrush
Breathed new life all around

STACCATO STABS

One Love
True Love
Big Love

(CHORUS)

I love this town, these lights, these fading streets
The City's soul, its heart, this life is sweet.
Beautiful woman, smile, please don't hide
Tell me your secrets, I stay by your side.

2.
My people seek redemption
No one listens to their song
On the winds I hear the echoes
(but) when I mend I feel strong

(CHORUS REPEAT)

SORAYA: You still haven't told me anything I don't know.

3.
One thing I broke – can't mend inside
My wife I lost, my tender heart has died
But life goes on
Deep lows and gentle highs
Heart beat slow

Life is fall
Life is rise
I try to live on

(CHORUS VARIATION)
I love this town, these lights, these fading streets
I found my role, to fix and mend my soul
Beautiful woman, why so shy?
Tell me your secrets, don't walk on by.

CAL: Now, it's your turn.

SORAYA: You wouldn't like what you heard.

CAL: Try me.
It was nice what you did for that young girl.

SORAYA: I didn't do it to be 'nice'. I did it because we need some fresh injection of talent, a new face, a different act. Sita has potential.

CAL: Of course, you're a business woman and you had no empathy with her situation.

SORAYA: My dear man, I have no idea who you think I am, but 'social worker' does not come into it.

CAL: My dear woman, you don't fool me.

SORAYA: You do know what I do for a living don't you? You haven't got me mixed up with Mother Theresa?

CAL: Tell me your story.

SCENE 6

(NB. In her 'Bollywood fantasies' something deeply personal about SORAYA's story comes out, so that the music and drama become the same thing. In a sense, these fantasies tell a Bollywood-style film within the musical. In this scene, SORAYA sings the first part of her story to CAL. In each of these fantasy numbers, another member of the cast plays SORAYA as a young woman).

We are transported into Bollywood magical past. The style of the songs are all from the past. This is the first of SORAYA's Bollywood fantasy scenes.

SORAYA: I grew up in a village in India where the lush green paddy fields stretch flat as far as the eye can see. We were poor farmers. But we had a good life.

We go back in time to SORAYA as a young girl. She is playing with her friends in the field. We create an Indian idyllic village life with the ensemble – farmers picking rice etc.

SORAYA: I had a very happy childhood. I played in the fields and the rivers with my friends, my mother always made sure we had enough to eat and my life was blessed with love.
But then my mother died and my father started to drink.

FATHER enters, drunk and angry. He grabs hold of (YOUNG) SORAYA by the hair and drags her screaming from her friends. Her friends and SORAYA are distraught at being separated.

FATHER: I can't keep you anymore. I can't look after you. Do you understand? Nearly fourteen now. You should be earning your own living.

SORAYA: Papa, Papa! Where are you taking me – no…no…I don't want to go…

FATHER marches her away from the village and throws SORAYA onto the floor at the feet of an elderly Indian woman (BINDI dressed up as SAMEENA BIBI). SORAYA looks up at the woman from the floor.

FATHER: This is Sameena Bibi.

SAMEENA BIBI: Let me look at you child.

SAMEENA BIBI cups SORAYA's face in her hands and inspects her.

SAMEENA BIBI: Very pretty. She'll do nicely.

SAMEENA BIBI hands over some money to FATHER. He looks satisfied and turns to SAMEENA BIBI. SORAYA rushes after him.

SORAYA: Papa! Please, don't leave me here.
Where are you going? What about my friends? Who will look after you?

FATHER stops, looks down at the crying SORAYA.

FATHER: Forgive me *Beti.* At least you will learn a trade here.

FATHER extricates himself from SORAYA and exits.

SAMEENA BIBI approaches and tries to comfort the crying SORAYA.

SAMEENA BIBI: Little one, don't cry.

SORAYA: I want my Papa!

SAMEENA BIBI: This is your home now. I will look after you.

SORAYA: I WANT TO GO HOME!

SAMEENA BIBI: You cannot go home – you are my child now.

SORAYA: I want my papa. He needs me to look after him.

SAMEENA BIBI: Shhh…please, child…I will take good care of you. I will teach you everything I know. How to coax with your eyes, plead with your body, how to sing like an angel and show love through your words.

But when you dance, that's when the gods themselves will peek out of the heavens to watch you and the goddesses will smart with envy.

A group of women enter, crowd around and start to dress the YOUNG SORAYA.

SAMEENA BIBI: I want you to be proud of your art. *Baijis* were mentioned in pre-Vedic texts and were refined women, they knew Urdu and Sanskrit, they were learned and intellectual and could entertain men with intelligent conversation; they taught the sons of kings and noblemen the etiquette of how to take *paan,* how to drink, even how to tie their shoes. They knew a thousand texts, they were educated and free, not subservient like wives. Soraya, you should always see yourself as equal to a man.

The room fills up with bejewelled men lounging on silk cushions. As the crowd of dressers part, the young SORAYA is transformed into a beautiful courtesan. All eyes are on her sat in the centre, dressed in silks and brocade performing to the men. Every man is enthralled and in the palm of her hand. She sings in a deep and husky voice, an old-fashioned song, using her eyes to make contact, making every man in the room feel special. She moves her body and uses her hands to express herself – sometimes coquettish, at others hurt or lovesick. CAL has never heard SORAYA's story and is entranced by what he sees and hears.

SONG FROM THE FILM 'UMRAO JAAN'
 – 'DIL CHEEZ KYA-HAI' (1981)

What is my heart?
Take my life
Just one time, listen to what I say
You come here again and again
You know these walls and doors intimately
I understand that friends don't supervise each other
But why do you take favours from a stranger?

What is my heart?
Take my life

If you ask me to
I'd bring down the sky to the ground for you
Nothing is difficult if you set your mind to it.
Just one time, listen to what I say
Listen, listen.

At the end when the Bollywood atmosphere has faded and we are back in the café, we end on CAL who looks stunned.

CAL: WOW!

SCENE 7

BINDI is eating a curry from a Tupperware box in front of the box dressed in her pyjamas.

SITA is sitting at the kitchen table on the laptop. She is sifting through some papers. KABIR enters. He hovers around her a little bashful.

SITA: Fauzia's business plan.

KABIR: They've got you working already?

SITA: It's nothing. Anyway, I'm good with figures. Want to finish college to be an accountant.

KABIR: Don't you want to be a dancer?

SITA: That too, but I gotta have a back-up plan. Everyone needs an accountant and Fauzia's trying to set up a hijab business.

KABIR: A what?

SITA: You know – head scarves for Muslim women? She's got some great ideas for designs. First though, she's gotta come up with a good name. 'Hijabi Heaven?…Hot Hijabs.' Or 'Hijabilicious!' What d'you think?

KABIR: Erm…yeah.

SITA: You're not much help.

KABIR: Not my area of expertise. Listen, where did you learn to sing and dance like that?

SITA: Me and me cousins. Used to watch all the old Indian films. I just practiced in front of the box…then later on me own in me bedroom.

KABIR: You seen much of London?

SITA shakes her head.

KABIR: You ever left home before?

SITA shakes her head.

KABIR: How did you make your way all the way down here?

SITA: I'm not little red riding hood. Just googled directions.

KABIR: Must have been scary.

SITA: Staying at home was scary.

KABIR: D'you miss them?

SITA: Not my parents, or me brothers. Glad to see the back of them. But my little sister. She's only ten.

KABIR: What's her name?

SITA: Rina. Can't believe I'll never see her again.

> *SITA breaks down and starts to sob.*

> *KABIR looks embarrassed but moved.*

KABIR: When it's all died down a bit, I'm sure…

SITA: I can't ever go back there. My brother – he'll kill me.

> *SITA cries some more.*

SITA: Rina looked so sad when I said goodbye. Begged me to take her with me.

KABIR: Come on…

SITA: Promised myself I wouldn't cry…
Ouch…

> *SITA has a paper cut.*

> *KABIR sits closer to SITA and takes her hand. He inspects it, takes a tissue from his pocket and wraps it round her finger.*

SITA: Bloody big bandage for a paper cut. You're a right wally. Now I look like sleeping bloody beauty.

> *SITA laughs but then relents.*

I wish my brothers were like you. You're so…

KABIR: What?

SITA: Kind.

You can be my new brother.

KABIR: I don't want to be your brother.

SITA: You can be my friend then.

KABIR: Don't want to be your friend.

SITA: Charming!

KABIR: Prince charming – yeah – I like that.

SITA: Stop looking at me that way.

KABIR: What way?

SITA: Like you want to kiss me.

KABIR: I don't want to kiss you.

SITA: Why not?

KABIR: I barely know you. And besides, that'd be a bit like taking advantage of you.

SITA: Yeah. You're right. So don't try any funny business.

KABIR: I won't.

They both sit in an awkward silence for a moment and then both turn to kiss each other at the same time. It's a long kiss. SITA quickly pulls away, suddenly embarrassed when OMAR enters.

Anyway, better get this to Fauzia.

SITA exits. She stops and turns before leaving.

KABIR has gone into a trance. OMAR snaps his fingers and waves his hands in front of KABIR's face.

OMAR: Woah! What's she done to you?

KABIR: I don't know but I feel...I feel...

OMAR: Kabir, didn't know you had it in you. Fast work!

OMAR slaps palms with KABIR.

KABIR: She's beautiful.

SONG

KABIR sings an excited upbeat love song.

As he sings, he rushes out into London, whizzing around, telling everyone he meets that he's fallen madly in love.

We see SITA in her bedroom. She is also singing the same song about KABIR so the song is a duet although KABIR and SITA can't hear the other's thoughts.

Sita Oh Sita

KABIR:

> *That girl's so fine*
> *She is simply divine*
> *Sita – oh – Sita*
> *Oh oh oh*
> *Heart's pounding fast*
> *Have I found love at last?*
> *Sita Oh Sita*
> *Oh oh oh*

KABIR in his frenzy bumps into PAVEL in the street, nearly knocking him off his ladder.

(Dialogue)

PAVEL: Careful crazy boy! You want kill me? You okay?

KABIR: Something's happened.

PAVEL: Good happening? Or bad happening?

KABIR: Amazing. A girl.

PAVEL: Ahhhh…

KABIR: She has these eyes…big…and long legs…and her voice…like honey!

PAVEL: She can walk, talk and see. That's a good start.

(SONG)

KABIR:
> Now that I'm woken
> World seems so fresh
> My love has spoken
> And I hear its song
> Eyes want her sight
> I don't want to sleep
> Heart wants her beat
> My soul wants to leap
> Let me run
> Feel the sun
> The pulse and flare
> Let us be
> Blissfully
> Eternal pair
> Sink in her sighs
> Drink in her smiles
> Soak in her charms
> Drown in her arms

CHORUS
> That girl's so fine
> She is simply divine
> Sita – oh – Sita
> Oh oh oh

> What's this I feel?
> Can't be wrong – is it real?
> Sita – Oh – Sita
> Ohhhh

SITA joins in.

SITA:

Is love coming?
Can I feel it grow?

KABIR:

This love is rising
I can feel the flow

SITA:

What is this churning?
What can I allow?

KABIR:

My luck is turning
I am ready now

TOGETHER:

Can we run
Feel the sun
The pulse and flare
Should we be
Blissfully
Eternal pair?
Sink in love sighs?
Drink in love smiles?
Soak in love charms?
Drown in love's arms?

CHORUS

SITA:

That boy is so sweet
Not a geek or a creep
Kabir – oh – my love
Ohhh

KABIR:

Heart's pounding fast

> *I have found love at last?*
> *Sita Oh Sita*
> *Oh Oh Oh*

SITA rushes out and bumps into MANSOOR taking a delivery.

(Dialogue)

MANSOOR: Oy watch it *Pagal*! (Crazy)

SITA: Isn't it a glorious day?

MANSOOR looks confused.

MANSOOR: Is it? Bit cold for this time of the year, if you ask me.

SITA: It's the sunniest, brightest, warmest day of the year. I can't stop smiling.

MANSOOR: Don't worry, you'll grow out of it.

SITA: I don't want to.

FAUZIA protectively pulls SITA away from MANSOOR.

MANSOOR eyes FAUZIA.

MANSOOR: *(Calls out.)* She's with you is she? I might have known. She's mad that one.

FAUZIA: 'Cos she's happy?

MANSOOR: Because she's in love. It's a mental illness.

CHORUS

We have a face off between a group of boys and girls who have joined in with the song.

BOYS:
> *Hey bro's on cloud nine*
> *He's got sex on his mind.*
> *Sita Oh, Sita*
> *Oh… Cheater!*

GIRLS:

> *Slow down Baby Sis*
> *Is he fit? Can he Kiss?*
> *Kabir, oh Kabir*
> *He might be queer.*

BOYS:

> *Does she go? Is she smart?*
> *Will she break your poor heart?*
> *Sita Oh, Sita*
> *How far will she go?*

GIRLS:

> *Got a car? Or a job?*
> *Can he cook? Does he slob?*
> *Kabir oh Kabir*
> *Is he sincere?*

KABIR takes over and sings the CHORUS again.

At the end of the song, BINDI is also dancing along.

She switches off the remote happily and goes to bed.

SCENE 8

MANSOOR is outside his shop. ANISH, a young Asian man approaches him. BINDI is walking by with a shopping bag. She eavesdrops.

ANISH: *Salaam waleikhum.*

MANSOOR: *Waleikhum salaam.*

ANISH: Beautiful day.

MANSOOR: Is it?

ANISH: Bright sunshine.

MANSOOR: I never see it.

ANISH: Brother, you need to open your eyes. By the way, name's Anish.

MANSOOR: Anish.

ANISH puts out his hand to MANSOOR to shake hands. MANSOOR eyes the gesture warily before briefly shaking hands.

ANISH: You been in this area long brother?

MANSOOR looks at ANISH suspiciously.

MANSOOR: I'm not your brother.

ANISH: Just being friendly. Not something you Londoners are used to, is it?

MANSOOR: Where are you from?

ANISH: Up north.

MANSOOR: Don't like the north.

ANISH laughs.

ANISH: I don't like the north much either – but we have to deal with what the Good Lord has granted us.
I bet you know everyone around here?

MANSOOR: More or less.

ANISH: I'm looking for some assistance brother.

MANSOOR: What sort of assistance?

ANISH: It's my sister.

ANISH pulls out a photograph from his pocket and shows it to MANSOOR. BINDI takes a look too.

ANISH: Perhaps you have seen her?

MANSOOR recognises SITA but covers this up. He shakes his head.

ANISH: Wicked place London is it?

MANSOOR: If you are looking for wickedness, you can find it wherever you want. Every place has its dark alleys.

ANISH: Please help me.

MANSOOR: I don't know you.

ANISH: You Londoners, so suspicious! Here I am, trying to engage you in a perfectly reasonable exchange, reaching out for a human response.

MANSOOR: Forgive me. You are right. I am being inhospitable.

ANISH: My sister disappeared a couple of nights ago. Only seventeen and the apple of my parents' eyes. Sweet, innocent and very vulnerable.

MANSOOR: What do you mean she disappeared?

ANISH: Had a tiff with me. Got all worked up and ran away. Said some nonsense about going to London.

MANSOOR: What is her name?

ANISH: Sita.

BINDI gasps.

MANSOOR: I'm sure she'll come home.

ANISH: What if she can't? What if she's been abducted by a modern day *Ravanna*? Held captive somewhere?

MANSOOR: I'm sorry but I don't recognise her.

ANISH: Can I leave this photo here with you?

MANSOOR: Of course, but what makes you think she's here? London's a big place.

ANISH: I checked out her google history on the computer. I found bus times to Stratford.
You see what worries me is that perhaps she has fallen in with the wrong type. You know what this country is like.

MANSOOR: I do.

ANISH: It doesn't take much to turn a young girl's head.

MANSOOR: Seventeen you say? She is a young adult then. All birds must fly the nest sometime – sadly – we must allow the young to find their own way.

ANISH: Yes but brother, our women need to be protected. There are bad men and women who would take advantage of her innocence.

MANSOOR: Be patient Anish. I am sure she will find her way back to you all.

ANISH: I am worried, very worried for her.

ANISH turns to go.

ANISH: Please tell people, there is a reward for any information. If it leads to her.
(Offhand.) A thousand pounds.

MANSOOR: That's a lot of money.

ANISH: My sister is very precious to my family.
If you see her, tell her that her baby sister – Rina – is crying for her.
Khuda Hafiz

MANSOOR: Khuda Hafiz.

ANISH exits the shop. MANSOOR looks worried.

BINDI looks worried too.

BINDI: I don't like the look of him. Up to no good. He's a *goonda* (thug), a *420* through and through!

But MANSOOR doesn't hear. BINDI sighs and leaves the shop. We follow BINDI back as she goes back to her house.

SCENE 9

BINDI sits in her armchair and snoozes. KABIR is there too. He sits in the corner of the room with some bookkeeping.

The Mujra girls are all rehearsing. OMAR is there too. SORAYA sits on a cushion and instructs the dancing girls.

SORAYA: Here at Wah! Wah! Girls, we aim to ease men's burdens, to throw off the heavy cloak of responsibility and shake off the spectre of despondency. We indulge men's senses with beautiful dancers. I want you to hold back and slowly build – to coax as opposed to forcing yourself on the audience. Think of the gravity of your movements, the hold of the body – the art of *Tharav.*

SORAYA demonstrates with her mudras (hand gestures) and her abhinaya (acting using her eyes and face).

FAUZIA demonstrates a few moves.

SITA watches.

SORAYA: Slowly, slowly…you see. Now Sita, you try.

SITA has a go.

SORAYA: Very nice. But more coyness, as if you are shy.

FAUZIA: Yeah right.

Everyone giggles.

SORAYA: *Chup!* No messing around here. Anita…

ANITA demonstrates a move.

SORAYA: You see how they dance with more grace when they hold back and slowly build rather than rushing in with flashy moves right from the beginning?

SITA: Soraya Bibi, can I ask, will I be expected to 'entertain' the clients afterwards?

SORAYA looks horrified.

SORAYA: *Chi! Chi! Chi!*

I do not run a brothel here. These are not vulgarly dressed Asian women offering titillating jerks to Bollywood numbers. Those kind of Mujra dancers have neither the musical tradition nor any classical dance steps to speak of. In the old days the *Baijis* knew how to entertain men through their conversation.

FAUZIA: You have to admit though Sorayaji, the way to a man's wallet is through his trousers.

SORAYA is furious.

SORAYA: Enough of your cheek Fauzia! That is not what I am doing here.

FAUZIA: Sorry Soraya Bibi.

SORAYA: I am teaching you how to perfect the Indian dance form for entertainment for everyone.

SITA: Do you dance Soraya Bibi?

SORAYA: I used to, not anymore.

SITA: Why not?

SORAYA: Because now I teach. Enough questions Sita! You try.

SITA does the move but this time she improvises something a little flashier, ending with a pirouette.

SORAYA: You're not listening to me…

SITA: Just trying something different.

SORAYA: You haven't learnt the basics yet.
You can't run before you can walk.

SITA: But Soraya Bibi, what you're teaching is from back in the day. We don't have to dance for men anymore. We could try just…dancing?

SORAYA: We don't dance for men.

SITA: All this coaxing and holding back and…

SORAYA looks furious. KABIR looks anxious.

SORAYA: And all this jingly jangly – shake your butt isn't for the boys?

SITA: 'Least it's not so subservient!

SORAYA: Subservient?

SITA: It's a statement – we're not afraid of our sexuality anymore.

SORAYA covers her ears in shame.

BINDI wakes up with a start.

SITA: All I'm saying, is try something new, something different. Sure, we're here to entertain but, we're in the 21st century Soraya. Women have moved on.

FAUZIA: She's got a point Soraya Bibi.

ANITA: Sisters are doing it for themselves.

SORAYA: Who do you think you are? You come here and start telling *me* how to dance?

SITA: Men have to take us on our terms as equals and this Mujra dance you teach, to me, it's all about flirtation and the art of pretence.

SORAYA: I am teaching you how to be a real woman – not a loud brash – I'm here for the taking – available flesh – look at me as I stick my fanny in your face-type.

SITA: What about what we like? We can build on the old and make something new. But I'm just expressing who I am.

SITA takes an old kathak dance form and does something new and exhilarating with it. FAUZIA, SHANTI and ANITA join in. This is an item dance number.

SORAYA (and BINDI) watches on impassively, arms folded and unimpressed. KABIR is loving it.

At the end of the dance SORAYA stands, stubborn and unbending.

SORAYA: The pure dance form of the *bhaijis* is sacred.

SITA: It belongs in the past.

SORAYA: My life's work is rubbish? You think you can destroy everything I've built up?

SITA: No! Soraya Bibi, you misunderstand me…

SORAYA: I understand you perfectly. Now pack your bags and get out.

BINDI leaps to her feet anxiously.

BINDI: Soraya ji! No! It's not safe for her out there.

SITA looks furious and upset. She turns to walk out but KABIR, FAUZIA, SHANTI and ANITA all try and stop her.

KABIR: Mum! You can't do this.

SORAYA: Watch me.

FAUZIA: Soraya Bibi, no. You can't send Sita away…she is just a little…hot-headed.

SHANTI: She is trying to improve what we do.

SITA: It's fine…Soraya Bibi feels I don't respect her, she's wrong but…

KABIR: Sita, apologise to mum.

ANITA: Please Soraya Bibi – she's young – impetuous.

SORAYA: And very manipulative.

SITA: I wanted to learn from you Soraya Bibi.

SORAYA: Then you should have kept your mouth firmly shut and not questioned me. This is still my establishment and I gave you a chance to learn something. You've blown it Sita. Now, get your things together and leave.

FAUZIA, ANITA and SHANTI look at SITA. SITA exits – the other girls all follow her out.

KABIR and SORAYA glare at each other.

KABIR: That was out of order mum. I can't believe you just did that!

SORAYA: Don't Kabir. I'm not in the mood. I gave her a chance, but she threw it back in my face.

KABIR: Sita's the best thing to have happened to this place in years. Why're you so scared of change?

SORAYA: Just because you have the hots for her, doesn't mean that I should give shelter to a traitor!

KABIR: You're a stubborn, cruel, bitter woman.

SORAYA: How dare you.

KABIR: You're a control freak mum. If Sita goes, I go.

SORAYA: GO THEN! Chase after that troublemaker. I'm not stopping you.

KABIR storms out.

SORAYA: You'll be back!

SORAYA looks upset.

SCENE 10

SITA is packing her bags in her bedroom. She is upset and angry. ANITA, FAUZIA and SHANTI burst in.

ANITA: You're mad to speak to Soraya Bibi like that!

SHANTI: You're amazing.

SITA: She hates me. And you lot weren't any help.

FAUZIA: That's not fair.

SITA: Why didn't you stick up for me?

ANITA: We did.

SHANTI: We tried but…

ANITA: Just apologise to her.

SHANTI: Beg forgiveness.

SITA: No! Why should I?

FAUZIA: Be practical. Where are you going to go?

SITA: I'll find somewhere.

FAUZIA: What? Like a bus shelter?

SITA: What is this hold Soraya has on you all?

FAUZIA: She took us in…

ANITA: Gave us a home.

SHANTI: She's always looked out for us.

ANITA, SHANTI and FAUZIA sing and dance.

SITA has a moment of self-doubt.

SITA: I've been stupid haven't I?

The three girls all look at SITA with empathy.

ANITA: You'll be alright. We're only a text away.

FAUZIA: Here, take this.

FAUZIA pulls out a wad of cash from her cleavage/stocking.

SITA: I can't!

FAUZIA: You'll need it.

SITA: Fauzia!

FAUZIA: You can pay me back one day.

SHANTI: You're like us.

FAUZIA: You're a survivor.

ANITA, SHANTI and FAUZIA sing and dance.

SHAKTI SONG!

1.
Go!
Don't look back
I left home
Got my life back on track.

Every night and every day
Mum was always far away
I left home and sleeping rough
No-thing felt safe
Somehow found my way to here
Dancing gave me something new
Soraya drove away my fear
Sister so true!

CHORUS/TOGETHER

We're here together
So much Stronger, wiser, yeah,
Survivors
Forever
Join us, join us, yeah
Beauty…freedom…truth now
Rise up, feel our power
Beauty…freedom…truth now
Face the future – Shakti now

2.
Raised
Full of fear
Every night, I could hear
Her cries rise.
Mother never tried to fight
Father's voice so full of hate

Feared I was the next in line –
That was my fate.
When I grew he turned on me
Father beat me black and blue
No one came to rescue me
Till I found you **(Indicating to all the girls.)**

CHORUS/TOGETHER

We're here, together
So much stronger, wiser, yeah
Survivors
Forever
Join us, join us, yeah
Beauty…freedom…truth now
Rise up – feel the power
Beauty…freedom…truth now
Female…power…Shakti now

3.
Feel there is love here
There is hope near
Sisters share here
Feel there is joy here
No despair near
Be as one here
Learn to be strong
Do your own sweet thing;
It's not so wrong
To just let your soul sing.

CHORUS/TOGETHER

We're here
Together
So much stronger, wiser, yeah
Survivors

Forever

Join us, join us, yeah

Beauty…freedom…truth now

Rise up – feel our power

Beauty…freedom…truth now

Face the future…Shakti now.

NB. Shakti is the concept, or personification, of divine feminine creative power, sometimes referred to as 'The Great Divine Mother' in Hinduism. On the earthly plane, Shakti most actively manifests through female embodiment and creativity/fertility.

By the end of the song, SITA has packed her bag. She hugs all the girls tearfully and leaves.

END OF ACT I.

ACT II

SCENE 1

We are outside in CAL and SORAYA's two adjoining back gardens.

CAL is working hard in his garden, fixing a fence. BINDI enters with a cup of tea and sits and savours the fresh air and sun. She dunks a biscuit. SORAYA is hanging out her washing. SORAYA watches CAL working for some time before he stops and looks up.

CAL: So, you chucked out the new girl?

SORAYA: You heard? Oh – I forgot – 'course – you know everything 'round here. She was…trouble.

CAL: Kabir said she's been through a lot.
Convinced that her family are all waiting out there to snatch her.

SORAYA: I don't know. Maybe. Maybe not. Could be making it all up just for some attention.
Kabir's gone as well.

CAL: I know. I found them both sleeping on a park bench last night.

SORAYA looks horrified.

SORAYA: He was with her?

CAL: You don't get it do you? They're in love Soraya. He won't leave her. It was freezing – so I brought them back to my place. I got a spare room.

SORAYA looks relieved and then upset.

SORAYA: You took them in? I was trying to teach them a lesson!

CAL: Why're you such a cow?

SORAYA: You don't understand.

CAL: Try me.

SORAYA: I made sacrifices. I built this place up on my own.
That Sita…

CAL: …is a vulnerable young woman and you know what this
city does to girls like her. It's dangerous.

SORAYA: Young people today expect everything to be handed
on a plate. They demand the world to bow to them. She
was trying to destroy my life's work! It's important to me.
Without it, my struggles are worthless.

CAL: I thought you cared about the girls? How could you be
so heartless?

SORAYA looks shocked.

SORAYA: No one helped me. My father abandoned me, no one
stood by me when I came here.

CAL: So what makes you different from your father? What the
hell happened to you Soraya?

SORAYA: I had to learn the hard way.

BINDI enters the next scene as SAMEENA BIBI.

SCENE 2

This is the second of SORAYA's Bollywood-style flashbacks.

*SAMEENA BIBI and the young SORAYA (SITA) enter. SAMEENA
combs and plaits the young girl's hair.*

SAMEENA BIBI: Tonight, my little one, you are to dance for
a very rich and famous man. You must wear the dress I
bought you for your birthday and tonight, you can wear
my pearls. I want you to look your best.

SORAYA: Sameena Bibi was like a mother to me.
She fed me, dressed me and took great care of me.

SORAYA: But Sameena Bibi…

SAMEENA BIBI: No buts. This is a great honour. He has asked for you. He has asked especially to see you dance.

SORAYA: Why me? Why not Nusrat or Jamila?

SAMEENA BIBI: Because my little one, your fame and beauty has already spread far.

SAMEENA BIBI places a string of pearls around SORAYA's neck.

SAMEENA BIBI: You have learnt well from me and have made me proud.

SORAYA: What is this man's name?

SAMEENA BIBI: His name is unimportant. What *is* important is that you make his pulse race and fill his heart with utter devotion to you.

SORAYA: What if I don't like him Sameena Bibi?

SAMEENA BIBI: That is not a question you can afford to ask little one. You will have to learn to like him.

SORAYA: What is he like?

SAMEENA BIBI: I can tell you this much. He is a rich, young man. Now, compose yourself, he is coming soon.

As the musicians and other dancers enter and prepare, SORAYA composes herself.

The young rich man enters and SORAYA dances a big Bollywood-style dance for him. Of course, the rich young man (TARIQ) can't take his eyes off SORAYA.

SONG AND DANCE – MAAR DAALA
FROM THE FILM DEVDAS (2002)

Whose footstep is this?
Whose shadow is this?
There was a knock at my heart;
who entered here?
Who spread this vibrant colour over me?
(maar Daala) I died from happiness
[lit.: my happiness killed me]
(maar Daala)… It killed me…
Who spread this vibrant colour over me?
(maar Daala) I died from happiness;
(maar Daala)… it killed me…
(allah maar Daala)… God, it killed me…
The moon did not decorate my palm,
nor did I contract any relationship with the stars.
Nor did I make any complaint of God…
I hid every sorrow;
with laughter I bore each injustice.
I even embraced thorns,
and was wounded by flowers.
Yes, but when I raised my hands in prayer,
I begged God for you!
God, I begged for you!

At the end of the dance, the entranced TARIQ takes SORAYA in his arms and kisses her.

As the Bollywood scene fades, CAL is left wanting more.

CAL: What happened next?

SORAYA: I became the rich man's lover.

CAL: And then what?

SORAYA laughs at CAL's eagerness.

CAL: Soraya! Tell me?

SORAYA: Three years. And of course I became pregnant.

CAL: Kabir?

The young SORAYA runs in crying. TARIQ charges in after her.

TARIQ: I can't, they won't let me Soraya. It's not me, it's my family.

SORAYA: Are you so weak-willed that you can't even fight for me or your child?

TARIQ: They will disown me. I will lose all my inheritance.

SORAYA: We don't need money. We have each other.

TARIQ: Don't be ridiculous Soraya.

SORAYA: You would throw me and your child aside, so you can keep face with your family?

TARIQ: I'm not throwing you aside and Sameena Bibi has said, she will find a good home for the baby when it's born.

SORAYA: What?

TARIQ: You will give your baby a better chance in life if you give it to a good family.

SORAYA: *(Horrified.)* How could I be so wrong about you?

TARIQ: I do love you Soraya. But we have to be practical…

SORAYA: If you loved me, you would marry me and be a father to this child.

TARIQ: Be realistic, face the facts. I can still see you, just as before. But I can't give you my name.

SORAYA: Yes, you are right. I must face facts. I *will* face the facts.

The young SORAYA looks calm and determined. TARIQ is a little thrown by her calmness.

She gives TARIQ one last look and then exits.

TARIQ: *(Calls out.)* Wait! Soraya? Where are you going?

TARIQ runs out after SORAYA. He catches her and drags her back. There is a dance routine as the two tussle and a fight breaks out.

He starts to beat her. SAMEENA BIBI enters. SORAYA runs to her and hides behind SAMEENA BIBI.

SAMEENA BIBI: Little one! Why are you fighting? This is your kismet, your destiny.

SORAYA: I don't want to give my baby away. I don't want to be his mistress.

TARIQ: What did you expect? That I would give everything up for you?

SORAYA: Please Sameena Bibi. I want to go home – to my father.

TARIQ: Home? You think your father wants you back now?

SAMEENA BIBI: There is nowhere else for you to go little one. Your father left town a while ago. And anyway, this is your home now.

SORAYA: My father wouldn't leave without telling me.

SAMEENA BIBI: He sobered up and has gone across the seas to seek his fortune – so they say.

SORAYA: Then I will make my own way. I will…ah!

TARIQ catches hold of SORAYA by the hair and drags her.

SAMEENA BIBI: Tariq Jee – there is no need for you to beat the poor girl.

TARIQ: You keep out of this you ugly old hag.
Soraya listen to me. You will stay here until your baby is born and then we will find someone to take your child. My sister is childless and she would welcome…

SORAYA: That will never happen.

TARIQ pulls out a knife and holds it to SORAYA's throat.

TARIQ: You will do as I say or I will cut your face up so badly, all men will avert their faces in disgust when they see you.

SORAYA: I thought you loved me.

TARIQ: My sister needs a child.

TARIQ plays with the knife.

TARIQ: Maybe I should make a few slices for insurance, that way you won't be able to go anywhere. Who would want a an ugly dancing girl?

SORAYA suddenly twists her body, taking TARIQ by surprise and grabs the knife plunging into TARIQ's chest. SAMEENA BIBI screams. TARIQ staggers back, blood pouring from his wound.

He looks at SORAYA in shock.

SAMEENA BIBI: *(To SORAYA.)* Get away from this place Soraya. Run…run away…

TARIQ collapses on the floor.

TARIQ: Help me…Sameena Bibi…

SORAYA stares down at her bloody hands, frozen to the spot.

SAMEENA BIBI: For the sake of your baby. Run for God's sake.

SAMEENA BIBI takes off her gold bangles, her necklace and other jewellery. She ties it hurriedly in a shawl and gives the bundle to SORAYA.

SAMEENA BIBI: GO NOW. SORAYA…SAVE YOURSELF!

(The younger) SORAYA turns and flees.

TARIQ lies on the floor, clutching the knife in his heart. He reaches his hand out to SAMEENA BIBI. SAMEENA sits down on a chair and watches TARIQ as he slowly bleeds to death.

The scene changes back into the back garden.

CAL: You killed him?

SORAYA: What you going to do? Call the Police?

CAL: No…no…but that's one hell of a thing to live with all this time.

SORAYA: It was self-defence!

CAL: I'm not judging you.

SORAYA: I don't care what you think.

CAL: Does Kabir know?

SORAYA: What do you think?

CAL: How can you have kept it a secret all these years?

SORAYA: I shouldn't have told you.

CAL: But you did. And I want to help you.

SORAYA: I don't need your help. This is none of your business.

CAL: What happened to Sameena Bibi?

SORAYA looks away. She is upset.

SORAYA: Don't ask me anymore Cal. Please. Leave it alone.

CAL: I want to know what happened next.

SORAYA turns to go back into her house.

CAL: Soraya. Don't turn me away.

SORAYA: I'm damaged goods Cal. You don't know half of what I've done.

CAL: Tell me, I want to know.

SORAYA: Sameena Bibi…she…she…confessed to murder. She took the blame for my act. They arrested her, tried her… she died in a stinking, filthy prison. Because of me.

CAL reaches out to try and hold SORAYA. SORAYA pushes him away.

SORAYA: There's nothing more to say on the subject.

CAL: I'm your friend Soraya.

SORAYA: I don't want your friendship.

CAL: Soraya…

SORAYA: Go away Cal, leave me alone.

CAL is torn. He wants to tell SORAYA he loves her but can't find the words. SORAYA rushes off. CAL looks on after SORAYA with longing.

SCENE 3

It is later – night time.

PAVEL enters and waits on the street corner with some paint pots. He calls out to CAL when he sees him.

PAVEL: Hey! Mr Cal!

CAL: Mr Pavel. What's up?

PAVEL: I have a decorating job for tonight. Cash up front. Brother-in-law is coming in a van.

CAL: Decorating at night?

PAVEL: A rich kid in Epping Forest. His parents are away, he has a party, the house gets trashed. Parents are coming back tomorrow morning.

CAL: Some party.

PAVEL: We have eight hours to fix the mess.
Now listen Cal, you are taking all of my business from me.

CAL: Am I?

PAVEL: People are always saying – 'Cal will do the job for me, Cal says he can do it as a favour'. You are undercutting me. So, I have plan. Why you not come and work for me? I give you a good cut of the profits.

CAL: Thanks. But no thanks.

PAVEL: Why not? You don't like that I am Polish?

CAL: I have nothing against the Polish.

PAVEL: Why then?

CAL: I worked hard for many years, employed people, had a good team.

PAVEL: What happened?

CAL: My wife died. I lost the hunger. Couldn't be bothered.

PAVEL: I am sorry man. Very sorry. When the heart is broken...

CAL: That was many years ago. Now, I like the fact that I have no responsibilities, no staff and all I have to do is earn enough through gardening to keep myself fed and with a roof over my head. I am happy.

PAVEL: Do me a favour. Next time, someone needs something doing, give them my card.

PAVEL pulls out a business card and hands it over to CAL.

CAL: Okay.

PAVEL: I still have the hunger. I have many mouths to feed and many roofs to keep over heads.

CAL: Good luck.

CAL shakes hands with PAVEL.

PAVEL reaches over to shake hands.

PAVEL: How're you doing? Looking like the whole world is balancing on your shoulders.

CAL: Just thinking.

PAVEL: Ahhh...I can tell, you are thinking deeply about a woman. Yes, yes. I am right!

CAL sucks his teeth.

PAVEL: Who is she?

CAL looks away.

PAVEL: She is playing with your feelings?

CAL: It's much more complicated than that.

PAVEL: Women! They are always complicated.
As the Polish saying goes: 'sex should be friendly.
Otherwise stick to mechanical toys. It's more sanitary'.

CAL looks confused. PAVEL laughs.

PAVEL: I am just joking with you man. Just joking! But is this
complicated woman worth the effort?

CAL: I don't want to have this conversation with you. It's late.
I'm on my way home.

PAVEL: Must be someone special – yes? To have turned Cal's
head upside down. You are always so…so…calm and
happy. Who is she?

CAL: Soraya.

PAVEL: *(Surprised.)* The lady who owns the dancing club?

CAL: Yes.

PAVEL: You like to watch her dancing for you?

CAL: No – it's not like that.

PAVEL: I have been in there – it's good dancing – respectable
place. Everywhere else is Polish girls dancing around poles.
Not nice. Makes a change.
You are in love – yes?

CAL: Yes…no…yes…

PAVEL: I see the problem. Confusion, fear…inability to face
your feelings. You should take my advice.

CAL: What?

PAVEL: This. If you love her, it's worth the effort.

CAL: Is that another Polish saying?

PAVEL: No, but this one is:
'Fear has big eyes'.

PAVEL sings a song to CAL.

'PAVEL'S SONG'

PAVEL:
In my home town girls are not so…pure
Some girls shine like pitch forks in…manure
Stop your wishy washy
It is easy peasy
Don't be pussy wussy
Try licking her face.

CHORUS
1.

Tell her your feelings
Stop you silly ravings
You have chance in life – be happy
Fling your pride aside
Reveal your mind, don't hide
Take your chance
To find some sweet romance

2.

The woman thinks you dandy
Stop your namby pamby
Desire burns bright for both your passions
kiss her mouth, her face
Man up, state your case
Take her in your arms
You'll get past first base

(Dialogue)

CAL: You make it sound so easy!

PAVEL: Love is easy. Complicated bit is recognizing your big feelings.

PAVEL:

> Nature's gift is given to the...youth
> But true art comes with age that's the...truth
> Dirty love, flirty love, get romanski
> Guilty love, filthy love, make advanski
> Thirsty love, bursty love, flexy love, sexy love get enhanski
> Buy some viagra.

CHORUS

3.

> Soraya is beauty
> You have manly duty
> Wipe the tears of fear from your eyes
> You must seize her tight
> Do not try to fight it.
> Why try to escape?
> Embrace your sweet fate.

4.

> Grab your courage
> Aim for marriage
> Love that girl with all your heart
> Pull up your best trousers
> Buy the girl some flowers
> Love her everyday
> Don't be so gay.

(Dialogue)

CAL: Maybe you're right. I should just tell her how I feel.

REPEAT of CHORUS 3 and 4 with CAL joining in.

SCENE 4

SITA is standing outside in the street with her bags. KABIR is with her.

KABIR: Let me talk to her.

SITA: I don't think she'll let me back in even if I do apologise.

KABIR: Mum pretends she's tough but underneath…just wait here.

> *KABIR kisses SITA.*

It'll be fine. Don't look so worried.

> *KABIR enters the house. SITA hangs around outside.*

> *SORAYA is sat at the kitchen table. She looks at KABIR and tries to hide her pleasure at seeing him again.*

SORAYA: You're back are you?

KABIR: Are you okay?

SORAYA: I can survive without you, you know.

KABIR: Sita wants to apologise.

SORAYA: She can't come back.

KABIR: You were the one that said I needed to find a new girlfriend.

SORAYA: There are so many pretty girls out there – why do you have to choose the one troublesome, screwed-up girl? What's wrong with a nice normal girl?

KABIR: Mum, if you wanted a normal girlfriend for me, you should have led a normal life. Got a job as a doctor's receptionist, or a supermarket cashier, not run an exotic dancing club.

SORAYA: But but you're falling in love.

KABIR: I've never felt like this before. She makes me feel… special.

SORAYA: Stop that feeling.

KABIR: When was the last time you actually loved someone?

SORAYA: I love you.

KABIR: Not me…a lover.

SORAYA: Your father.

KABIR: You never talk about him.

SORAYA: It still upsets me even to think about it.

KABIR: Don't you want me to be happy Ma? To find and love someone special?

SORAYA: It's a dangerous thing.

KABIR: Dangerous? Ma, just because you closed yourself off, doesn't mean that I should too.

SORAYA and KABIR'S SONG
– 'Don't Fall For Love'

SORAYA:

> *Safe in my arms*
> *Far from life's harms*
> *You are my charm.*
> *Always my constant one*
> *Stars, the moon, the earth, my sun –*
> *My planet.*
> *Breathed life into your soul*
> *Gave you love, Made you whole*
> *I'll keep you safe and sound*
> *In this life of pain and gain*
> *Through the wild worlds all around*
> *I'll guide you.*
> *Don't trust a lover's vows,*
> *Don't last beyond their tease*
> *Like lies and sighs they blow away with wind or softest breeze.*

Mother's love endures through time
Your heart and hers, sublime
Lover's love slips slides away to leave you stumbling

SORAYA:

Don't fall for love
Love makes you lose your senses.
Don't fall for love
Love leaves your heart defenceless.

KABIR:

Safe in her arms
Far from life's harms
She brings me calm.
Sita is my constant one
Stars, the moon, the earth, my sun –
My planet.
Breathes life into my soul
Gives me love, makes me whole
She keeps me safe and sound
In this life of pain and gain
Through the wild worlds all around
She'll guide me.

SORAYA:

> *Don't trust a lover's vows,*
> *Don't last beyond their tease*
> *Like lies and sighs they blow away*
> *With wind or softest breeze.*
> *Mother's love endures through time*
> *Your heart and hers, sublime*
> *Lover's love slip-slides away to leave you stumbling*

KABIR:

> *I'll fall for love*
> *Love touches all my senses.*
> *I'll fall for love*
> *I thrill to feel defenceless.*

SITA:

> *I love you too*
> *Love your eyes*
> *Love your heart*
> *Love your*
> *Soul*
> *My Kabir*
> *I'm free from fear*
> *Trust my word*
> *In your arms*
> *I feel whole*
> *Be my world.*

SITA and KABIR:

> *I'll fall for love*
> *Love touches all my senses.*
> *I'll fall for love*
> *I thrill to feel defenceless.*

SCENE 5

*BINDI is out on her own walking. She walks past MANSOOR's shop –
the 'DELUXE-DHOBI-WALLAH' is hanging off its hinges. She notices
that BAILIFFS are busy carting MANSOOR's things out of his shop.
BINDI looks at MANSOOR shocked.*

MANSOOR: No! No! Not my washing machine! You can't do
    this…no…please…it's my life's work…just give me some
    more time.

BAILIFF: Sorry mate. You run out of time.

> *As MANSOOR is left with nothing. He sits on the steps, distraught.*

BINDI: Mansoor *bhai*? What has happened?

MANSOOR: I'm bankrupt. I'm a washed-up – has-been.

SCENE 6

*SORAYA sits on her own in the Mujra. She looks thoughtful. CAL
enters.*

SORAYA looks up surprised to see him.

CAL: You alright?

SORAYA: Fine.

> *There is an awkward silence and CAL turns to go.*

CAL: Okay I'll go then.

SORAYA: Cal – wait.

> *CAL hovers uncertain.*

SORAYA: You were kind and understanding and you
    listened to me. All I did was…it wasn't right…
    I'm sorry.

CAL: I keep trying to tell you woman, I'm your friend.

SORAYA: I know. I missed you.

CAL: It's only been three days.

SORAYA smiles.

SORAYA: Three long days.

CAL: Felt like a year.

SORAYA motions for CAL to sit down.

SORAYA: This is the first time you've ever come in to my house.

CAL hesitates.

CAL: Not going to bite my head off, are you?

A persistent knocking on the door shatters the moment.

MANSOOR rushes in followed closely by KABIR.

KABIR: Mum, he insisted, just barged past me…

SORAYA is flabbergasted to see him.

MANSOOR: Soraya – my darling…

SORAYA: Since when have I been your 'darling'?

MANSOOR: I wanted to ask…to beg…

SORAYA: I am not interested.

CAL: Mansoor, what's going on?

MANSOOR falls to his knees at SORAYA's feet. She looks appalled.

MANSOOR: I've lost everything. I couldn't pay the bills. They've closed me down. After all those years! I have nothing, no one, nowhere. I'm finished.

KABIR: What's that got to do with us? Think we care about you?

MANSOOR: Soraya – I need your help.

SORAYA: Of course you do. Why else would you be here grovelling at my feet. You want me to bail you out? Forget it.

SITA, FAUZIA, ANITA and SHANTI all enter and watch.

MANSOOR: Please, I beg you.

SORAYA: Ask your sons.

MANSOOR: You know they abandoned me.

SORAYA: Ask your wife.

MANSOOR: She left me too. Stop torturing me!

CAL: Mansoor man, how can you come here and ask Soraya to help you…surely?

KABIR: Get out.

MANSOOR: I have nowhere else to turn. She is my one last hope.

CAL looks utterly confused. He tries to help MANSOOR up who has fallen to the floor.

CAL: Come on old man – let me see you out.

MANSOOR: Kabir, she won't tell you but – we are blood.

SORAYA: Stop this nonsense!

KABIR: What does he mean?

SORAYA: Go home, Mansoor…

MANSOOR: I'm your mother's father. Your grandfather.

SORAYA: No…he's lying!

KABIR: Mum? What the hell is he talking about…?

SORAYA: He's crazy.

MANSOOR: Soraya, Tell him. He should know.

KABIR: Mum?

SORAYA looks from KABIR to CAL. She realises the game is up.

SORAYA: Cal, Kabir. Let me introduce you. This is my beloved, noble, affectionate father.

CAL looks amazed. KABIR looks lost.

CAL: Mansoor?

MANSOOR: It's true, I am her father, your grandfather. We have been estranged but now…things can be different.

SORAYA'S SONG 'SHAME'

INTRO

(Dialogue)

SORAYA: How dare you try and barge into my life again. After what you did to me. I was just a kid when you sold me off like a piece of baggage.

KABIR: What's this all about mum?

SORAYA: I'll tell you Kabir what your grandfather did.

SORAYA SINGS:

My sweet Ma –
She died so young
Left this world –
Her life unsung
No time to play
For love I prayed
Papa drank our life away!

CHORUS

You come here on your knees
You scum, you piece of sleaze
You never did me right
You sold my body to the night.
Shame!
Shame!

Shame on your wicked soul
Damn!
Damn!
Damn you to hell
I travelled here –
To set things right
Dreaming that –
You'd clasp me tight
I felt a fool
You were so cruel
Showed me the door
and called me 'whore'!

CHORUS

You come here on your knees
You scum, you piece of sleaze
You never did me right
You sold my body to the night.
Shame
Shame
Shame on your wicked soul
Damn
Damn
Damn you to hell

My mother's voice
So gentle to me
The warmth of memory
So long ago

Such love I knew
Through childhood days
With her life was true
Now just haze.

(Dialogue)

KABIR: Mansoor, is this true?

MANSOOR: I had my family honour to think of. I had a new family! It was wrong I know.

SORAYA: That's why I bought this place right under your nose so that you would never be able to forget me. Despite you, I made something of my life.

MANSOOR: I will make it up to you. We can be a family again.

SORAYA SINGS:

CHORUS

You gave me no protection
I yearned for your affection
You broke my heart in pieces
Escaped across the seven seas
Shame!
Shame!
Shame on your wicked soul
Damn!
Damn!
Damn you to hell!

Now get out.

MANSOOR is humiliated at having to beg and seething with anger gets up. As he is leaving, he sees SITA. He stops for a moment, looks at her and then exits. KABIR turns to SORAYA.

KABIR: My grandfather?

SORAYA: He rejected us both. I wanted to spare you the pain.

KABIR: Don't you think I had a right to know? We've been living opposite him all these years? For as long as I can remember?

SORAYA turns away. CAL watches both mother and son.

KABIR: You just wanted me to yourself didn't you? No aunts, no uncles, no cousins or brothers and sisters, no family – just me and you.

SORAYA: He's a good for nothing. He hates everyone.

KABIR: What else haven't you told me?

SORAYA turns away.

KABIR: Who was my father?

SORAYA is silent.

KABIR: You never, ever talk about him. Always avoid the question. What happened to him?

SORAYA: I told you, he died.

KABIR: How?

SORAYA: It was an accident.

KABIR: Who was my father?

SORAYA: He was a wealthy landowner. I was his mistress. When I refused to give you up, he tried to cut my face.

SORAYA falls silent. KABIR looks upset. SITA approaches KABIR and tries to pull him away.

SITA: Kabir, I don't think you should ask any more questions.

KABIR: What happened?
Mum, what the hell happened? Tell me.

SORAYA: He wanted to take you away from me.

KABIR: Tell me the truth.

SORAYA: This is the truth.

SITA: Kabir…

KABIR: I want to know.

SORAYA: It was self-defence.

KABIR: Tell me!

SORAYA: I killed him!

KABIR looks devastated. He rushes towards SORAYA.

KABIR: You heartless bitch.

SITA stands between SORAYA and KABIR.

SITA: No Kabir, she's your mother. What you gonna do? Hit her? You're no better than my brother.

KABIR exits, looks devastated and torn. He runs out.

SITA puts her arms around SORAYA who sobs.

SCENE 7

BUS STOP.

ANISH is sat at the bus stop . He is listening to his iPod and singing along with a hindi film song 'Mehbooba'. He has a rucksack on his back. We see from his demeanour, that far from being a nice brother, concerned for the safety of his sister, he is like the bandit Gabbar Singh in the film 'Sholay' – evil personified.

MANSOOR enters. He also has all his belongings in a rucksack.

ANISH: Ah – brother! Come and sit down!

ANISH leers at a couple of women who walk by and wolf whistles.

ANISH: Hello darling!

WOMAN: Get lost creep.

ANISH: *(Calls back.)* Racist! Islamaphobe!

MANSOOR: You're not even Muslim.

ANISH: She doesn't know though.

ANISH stands up and sings another bit from Mehbooba.

ANISH: You know the film brother? Sholay? My favourite.
And Helen in it – so voluptuous. They don't make 'em like
that anymore.

MANSOOR looks away.

ANISH: I wanted to be fillims. Once acted in a school play.
I was Toad of Toad Hall. And my teacher said I had
'potential'. Said I was a real drama queen – I think
she meant king but…my parents wouldn't let me. I
was desperate to go to these acting classes on Saturday
mornings – but no – parents said that it was a waste of
time. I could have been a Sharukh Khan.

You look troubled. Everything okay?

MANSOOR: Everything is lost.

MANSOOR sits down and covers his face.

MANSOOR: Have you seen your sister?

ANISH: Still no luck. No one has seen her, no one. It's like she
vanished into thin air.
In a puff of smoke.
Some whiskey?

ANISH produces a small bottle from his pocket.

MANSOOR: No, thank you. I don't…

ANISH: Good stuff, Johnny Walker.
You look like you could do with a…

MANSOOR: No, really. I used to…but not anymore.

ANISH: I see. I won't tempt you then.

*ANISH takes a sip and then keeps the bottle ostentatiously next
to MANSOOR.*

ANISH: I can't believe her nerve! To run away like that. Left
a note saying she wanted to dance and be free! Imagine.
Dancing is for loose women.

83

MANSOOR: Equality, that's what they've learned here.

ANISH: Back home, women know their place.

MANSOOR: It's the *laithi* if they misbehave.

MANSOOR reaches for the bottle of whiskey and starts to drink.

ANISH: None of this telling their men what they want all the time.

MANSOOR: It's changed back home too. Nowadays, even the Indian women in the village form collectives.

ANISH: What's the world coming to? Soon, we'll be taken over by these women.

MANSOOR: They'll put us in factories.

ANISH: I read in the newspaper – they say they don't need men anymore. To make babies, they just bottle our – you know – in a test tube and stick it inside the woman. *Phat a phat – baas* – a baby! Without the fun or all our hard work.

MANSOOR: That will never happen.

MANSOOR is gulping down the whiskey. BINDI enters (with a rucksack on her back too) she sits at the bus shelter.

ANISH: It *could* happen. If all the world was ruled by Anne Widdecombe types. Imagine that!

MANSOOR: She dances too doesn't she? Prostitute. Terrible, horrible…

ANISH: Then they would put us in factories.

MANSOOR: *Bhaiya* what bloody newspaper are you reading?

ANISH: The *Daily Mail.* It's a good paper. Always talks good sense.

ANISH: Then the men in the world will form an army and we will kill all those women who dare to try and put us in a factory.

MANSOOR: But if we kill all the women – how will we make babies? If we don't have babies – that's the end to human beings.

ANISH: We won't kill them all. We will put *them* in factories. Make them into our slaves.

MANSOOR: Ahhhh…very good.

But you know, it's not a very nice prospect is it?

ANISH: What?

MANSOOR: Armies, killing, women as slaves…what about our mothers? Our sisters? Our daughters?

Would they be slaves too? Not a pretty picture you're painting.

ANISH: Hmmm…

MANSOOR: I am just logically following your line of argument.

MANSOOR is drunk.

MANSOOR: I know where your sister is hiding. But first, I want the reward.

BINDI: No Mansoor!

ANISH: How do you know it's her?

MANSOOR: I've seen her.

ANISH: Really?

MANSOOR: With my own eyes.

ANISH: Tell me brother.

MANSOOR: Cash up front.

BINDI can't contain herself any longer.

BINDI: No Mansoor bhai! Don't sell your soul to the devil!

ANISH: I don't carry that sort of money around with me. Tell me first and then tomorrow I can get the cash for you.

MANSOOR: No deal.

ANISH grabs MANSOOR and holds him aggressively.

ANISH: Greedy little bastard.

MANSOOR winces but stays his ground.

MANSOOR: You offered the reward for information. Are you a man of your word?

ANISH throws MANSOOR back roughly and exits.

ANISH: Wait here. I'll be back with the cash.

BINDI rushes back to the Mujra. She shouts as she runs.

BINDI: Soraya Bi Bi! Kabir! Be Careful!

SCENE 8

BINDI rushes in to SITA's bedroom first. She tries to wave at them to warn them but they can't see her.

We are in SITA's bedroom with SITA, FAUZIA, SHANTI and ANITA.

FAUZIA: It's incredible that we lived so close to Mansoor all these years and…

ANITA: I never had a clue.

SHANTI: Makes sense – kind've. Him and Soraya Bibi always had it in for each other.

FAUZIA: How's Kabir?

SITA: He's upset – he's talked to his mum – they've made up but, it were a bit of a shock.

ANITA: You two are so loved-up.

FAUZIA: Sick making.

SITA: I love him. And he loves me.

ANITA: Sweet.

SITA: I think this is it. Kabir is the one!

FAUZIA: Don't get carried away. Love only lasts for three years, so make the most of it.

The others all hit FAUZIA and laugh.

ANITA: Don't judge everyone by your own standards.

SHANTI: Fauzia, you never last more than three weeks!

FAUZIA: That's not true. And actually, I'm waiting for my boyfriend to whisk me away from here. Any day now.

ANITA: Dream on Fauzia.

FAUZIA: Wait and see, this one will be different.

SHANTI: Yeah, yeah…

SITA: Anyway, you're my crew now. We'll keep in touch.

SHANTI and ANITA hug SITA.

FAUZIA: It's been cool, but I don't go all 'von Trapp' on me. I'm not gonna start wearing matching curtain salwaars with you or anything.

We hear the shattering of glass and ANISH jumps in through the window. FAUZIA, SHANTI and ANITA scream. SITA is stunned to see ANISH but stands her ground.

SITA: Anish!

ANISH: Knew I'd find you eventually.

SITA: Get out.

ANISH: Thought you could just run away?

SITA: What's it to you Anish? Why d'you care?

ANISH: Because, this is not the way things are done.

SITA: Get lost Anish!

ANISH looks around at the women.

ANISH: Nice…

FAUZIA: Get out of here – scum.

ANISH: She's mouthy this one isn't she? Friend of yours Sita?

SITA: Anish, leave me alone.

ANISH: Can't do that Sita. We have our family honour to think about.

SITA: What about our family honour when you go around beating people up, getting drunk, smashing things, stealing…? I'm not the one who ended up serving time for…

ANISH: Shut up. This isn't about me, this is about you.

SITA: You don't scare me anymore.

ANISH: Why don't you come home. Rina cries for you every day. Asks when you're coming back.

SITA: Don't use Rina.

ANITA starts to scream.

ANITA: Soraya Bibi! Kabir!

ANISH grabs hold of ANITA and holds her around the neck.

ANISH: One more sound from you, you little tart…

SHANTI: Don't you dare hurt her!

SITA: I'm not coming home.

ANISH: You wanna run from me all your life?

SITA: Leave me alone so I can get on with being happy.

ANISH: And you're happy here are you?
Whoring for a living?

SITA: I'm no whore.

ANISH: You look like one. All of you. Slags.
Some kinda weird nautch girls – dancing for a living?
Flashing your tits for dirty old men?

SITA tries to run for the door but ANISH is quicker. He makes a grab for her and slaps her. The he holds his hand over her mouth. There's a struggle but ANISH is stronger. All the women jump on.

ANISH: Either you come home with me now. Or I'm going to have to teach you a lesson.

ANISH pulls out a knife and holds it to SITA's neck. SITA stops struggling, afraid of the blade.

ANISH: Thought that would shut you up.

The door flies open and MANSOOR and KABIR enter. There is a stand-off.

ANISH: Ah here's the kind brother who sold you to me.

KABIR: *(Looking at MANSOOR.)* You!

MANSOOR: Put the knife down Anish.

ANISH: The best way to deal with cancer is to cut it out once and for all.

ANISH raises the knife but MANSOOR lunges at him. There is a struggle. SITA manages to get away and runs to KABIR. SORAYA enters and screams. ANISH stabs MANSOOR. When MANSOOR collapses, ANISH sees the blood on his hands and escapes.

BINDI: *NEHI-I-I-I-I-I!*

SORAYA rushes over to MANSOOR and holds him. MANSOOR is fading fast.

MANSOOR: Forgive me Soraya.

SORAYA: Hold on Papa…

Kabir, phone for an ambulance.

MANSOOR: I made a terrible mistake. I should never have sold you. Such a little girl. I was a monster…

SORAYA: Keep conscious, just focus on me…we'll get you through.

MANSOOR: Forgive me.

SORAYA: I forgive you Papa.

> *MANSOOR puts up his hand to SORAYA's cheek and then dies.*

> *SORAYA cries.*

> *As MANSOOR dies in SORAYA's arms we have a choral version of Mansoor's song 'Yah Allah!' with the entire ensemble singing.*

SCENE 9

Time passes.

We are back in the Mujra but now it is bare and empty. No more chairs or cushions. FAUZIA, SHANTI and ANITA enter. They are no longer dressed as dancing girls but in casual everyday clothes. Each carries a suitcase. They all look around the room.

SITA and KABIR enter too, both carrying cases. All five hug each other and say their farewells.

SORAYA enters.

FAUZIA: Soraya Bibi…

SORAYA: Good luck, all of you.

ANITA: Can't believe…

SORAYA: Anita, don't start crying, please.

SHANTI: Oh Soraya Bibi…

SORAYA: Kabir was right, this place belongs in another time. None of us can continue here, not after what happened. Just promise me, none of you will end up dancing in one of those terrible Mujra clubs?

FAUZIA: I'm going to live with my boyfriend. Although, if he misbehaves just once, I'm going my own way. He says he's going to help set up my business.

SHANTI: Me and Anita found a place and a job. We've got our own stall in the market.

SORAYA: What are you selling?

ANITA and SHANTI produce some under garments and hold them up.

ANITA: Tie-dyed Olympic lingerie – to start with anyway.

FAUZIA, SHANTI and ANITA all gather around SORAYA and hug and kiss her.

SORAYA: Stay in touch.

FAUZIA, SHANTI and ANITA all exit.

KABIR, SITA and SORAYA are left together. They stare at each other.

SITA: This time, I'm going back to college, finish that accountancy course.

SORAYA: Sita, I knew you were trouble from the moment I set eyes on you.

SITA: Come with us.

SORAYA: You really do not want me hanging around you both. Go. With my blessing.

KABIR: I love you Mum.

SORAYA: Look after each other.

KABIR gives his mum one last and long hug and then tears himself away.

SORAYA is left on her own. She sits in the big empty room on her own. The lights dim. CAL enters. He stands and watches her for a while and then approaches her and sits next to her.

CAL: So you sold the place?

SORAYA: Council bought it off me.

CAL: What happens next?

SORAYA: End of all my stories Cal. Nothing left to tell.

CAL: You gotta stop living in a fantasy world Soraya.

SORAYA: Reality's hard.

CAL: Yeah, but you know what? It's exciting.
Never know what's around the corner.
You don't have to entertain anyone anymore, you don't have to pretend or hide. Got no responsibilities, just have to look after yourself and enjoy your life.

SORAYA: I'm free.

CAL: To be yourself.

SORAYA: I'm afraid.

CAL: Don't be. I'm here. I was always here.

SORAYA: Missed you.

CAL: It's only been a few weeks.

SORAYA: Felt like a year.

CAL: Felt like two.

They both laugh.

CAL: I was waiting for you to come and find me.

SORAYA: Not my style.

CAL: Ohh that's right, you don't chase do you?

Beat.

CAL: I'll show you my heart if you show me yours?

SORAYA: Deal.

CAL: Soraya Bibi – I love you. And will cherish and stand by your side, if you'll have me.

SORAYA doesn't say anything. She walks away from CAL. CAL looks a little worried until he realises that SORAYA is going to sing for him.

As CAL sits back, finally SORAYA dances and sings for him. CAL is entranced.

SONG FROM THE FILM
'UMRAO JAAN' – 'DIL CHEEZ KYA-HAI' (1981)

What is my heart?
Take my life

Just one time, listen to what I say
You come here again and again
You know these walls and doors intimately
I understand that friends don't supervise each other
But why do you take favours from a stranger?

What is my heart?
Take my life

If you ask me to
I'd bring down the sky to the ground for you
Nothing is difficult if you set your mind to it.
Just one time, listen to what I say
Listen, listen.

EPILOGUE

BINDI gets out a newspaper and sits down to read it.

MANNY enters with a bag and some dry cleaning.

BINDI: Ah! You're back early. How was the conference?

MANNY: Not bad. Interesting papers but the food was third-class. These caterers – they always try to pretend to make a curry – thai, jungle, south Indian even curry goat and rice and peas – all tastes the same. Bland.

MANNY sits down.

MANNY: Nothing like my home cooking, what have you been eating?

BINDI: Without the master chef – to be honest – *hiji biji*. Supermarket microwave curries.

MANNY: Euch. Don't worry, I'm home now. We'll feast tonight. What have you been doing?

BINDI: Watched a fillim or two…or three…

MANNY: Which ones?

BINDI: Devdas… Umrao Jaan…
Beautiful women, sequins, dancing, songs, villains, murder, long-lost fathers, romance, made me cry.

MANNY: Have you written your paper?

BINDI: No.

MANNY: Watching fillims instead of working?

BINDI: It can wait.

MANNY: Baap reh Doctor Bindi Shah! What is the matter with you? You have to present your thesis on areas of DNA that govern the body's production of the protein Galanin. The whole faculty is coming to hear you speak next Thursday!

This is your groundbreaking work! Have you written a single word?

BINDI: It will come. Manny – can I ask you something?

MANNY: What?

BINDI: Do you love me?

MANNY looks at BINDI aghast.

MANNY: What?

BINDI: You heard me.

MANNY shakes his head.

BINDI: Manny?

MANNY: How can you ask me such a question? It's obvious. Isn't it? I adore you. I worship the dust beneath your feet. Always have, always will.

BINDI giggles.

MANNY: You are my Nargis.

BINDI: And you are my Dilip Kumar.

MANNY and BINDI embrace each other.

FAUZIA, ANITA and SHANTI all re enter with the rest of the cast as they MC a walk down.

FAUZIA, SHANTI and ANITA all MC the last walk down.

(Introducing OMAR and DEVI.)

FAUZIA: Omar moves are as good as it gets
He says it all with his pirouettes.

India's voice is given wings –
Angels rising when she sings.

(Introducing ANISH and PAVEL.)

FAUZIA: Give it up give it up
    for the Pole at the top
    Respect the man with a plan
    Works all hours,
    'til he flops.

ANITA: No more joy, for Anish
    He will never find peace
    Wherever he may range
    He simply cannot change

(Introducing BINDI and MANNY.)

SHANTI: Old gyal, clever bird
    Watches flicks, studies hard,
    You'd never guess on a bus
    She's bigger brained that all of us

FAUZIA: Grumpy man, take a bow
    Let Bindi show you how
    Past mistakes, hunt him down
    But this can be Mansoor's town

(Introducing SITA and KABIR.)

ANITA: Sita Sistah,
    No man can resist yah
    Taking your chances,
    With your dances
    Seize the day, seize the hour
    Rise up, rise up feel the power!

SHANTI: Sweet Kabir, loyal son
    Now's the time to have some fun
    Big respect you did your time
    Go with Sita, you'll be fine

(Introducing CAL and SORAYA.)

FAUZIA: Cal's the man
    A golden nugget
    In this world of oafs and muppets
    Faced his doubts, snatched his dream
    Now he basks in Soraya's beams

SHANTI: Give it up, Give it up
    Woman hood crawled to the top
    Glorious Soraya
    Our sweetest sistah
    Free at last from neglect
    Free at last, big respect.

    SORAYA introduces ANITA, FAUZIA and SHANTI.

SORAYA: Last but not least, never forgotten

    Beauty and brains, from top to bottom

    Anita and Shanti, East End pearls
    With queen Fauzia: the Wah Wah girls.

SONG WAH! WAH! GIRLS FINAL REPRISE

ANISH – I run from the police, live in hiding and lies
PAVEL – London town may be big – but the cops have big eyes.
SITA – I live for your love – my rising heart fills with joy
KABIR – This city lifting us up, our life time to enjoy

CHORUS

Wah! Wah! They call as we dance and we sing
Ghungrus ringing, bodies swaying
hands show love's glory, eyes burn our yearning
Dazzling, twirling, love-defining.

Wah! Wah! They call as we dance and we sing
Ghungrus ringing, bodies swaying
eyes set hearts racing, smiles bring men gasping
Whirling freely, life-affirming.

BINDI – I watch all my shows, love dreams, fantasies
MANSOOR – Laundrettes may seem dull– but my wife has the keys
SITA & KABIR – We live for our love – rising hearts filled with joy
This city lifting us up, our lifetimes to enjoy

CHORUS

CAL – We are old for love – but ancient dreams will not die
We can navigate life without starry eyes.
SORAYA – Not too old for new love – this time we must seize
Together we can build life and new memories.

CHORUS

The End.

GLOSSARY OF HINDI TERMS IN WAH! WAH! GIRLS

WAH WAH!	Wow/well done. Called out by an audience to show their appreciation.
SALAAM	Muslim term of greeting. Means 'peace'. Usually said with a salute.
NAMASTE	Indian term of greeting. Means, 'I bow to you'. With palms together, fingers upwards.
BETA	Son/young man/little boy.
BETI	Daughter/young woman/little girl.
(SORAYA/SAMEENA)	
BIBI/JI	Respectful title for a woman.
HIJAB	Muslim woman's head scarf.
PAGAL	Mad.
SALAAM VALEIKHUM	Muslim greeting – 'peace be upon you'.
VALEIKHUM ALAAM	Muslim response – 'And may peace be upon you'.
RAVANNA	The mythological 10 headed demon god who stole Sita from Rama.
GOONDA	Thug.
420	Literally Indian penal code for cheating and dishonesty. Calling someone a '420' means they are a crook or a con artist.
HUDA HAFIZ	Muslim parting term. Means 'Goodbye' or 'may God be your guide'.
THARAV	The rhythm of the dance.
CHI CHI CHI	A term to show one's disgust or disapproval.

BAIJIS	Indian courtesan.
SHAKTI	Divine female power and strength.
KISMET	Destiny.
NAUTCH girl	Dancing girl from Mughal times.
LAITHI	A large stick.
PHAT A PHAT	A phrase meaning 'quickly, quickly'.
BAAS	Enough/finished.
BHAIYA	Little brother.
BHAI	Brother.
HIJI BIJI	A phrase meaning 'rubbish'.
MERE JAAN	Term of endearment. My life/my heart/my love.

OTHER TANIKA GUPTA TITLES

Tanika Gupta: Political Plays
(Gladiator Games, Sanctuary, Sugar Mummies and White Boy)
9781849432474

Fragile Land
9781840023671

Inside Out
9781840023527

Meet the Mukhejees
9781840028614

ADAPTATIONS

The Country Wife
Based on William Wycherley
9781840025163

Great Expectations
Based on Charles Dickens
9781849431224

Hobson's Choice
Based on Harold Brighouse
9781840023831

WWW.OBERONBOOKS.COM

Follow us on www.twitter.com/@oberonbooks
& www.facebook.com/oberonbook